Dear Parent:
Your child's love of reading starts here!

Every child learns to read in a different way and at his or her own speed. You can help your young reader improve and become more confident by encouraging his or her own interests and abilities. You can also guide your child's spiritual development by reading stories with biblical values and Bible stories, like I Can Read! books published by Zonderkidz. From books your child reads with you to the first books he or she reads alone, there are I Can Read! books for every stage of reading:

SHARED READING
Basic language, word repetition, and whimsical illustrations, ideal for sharing with your emergent reader.

BEGINNING READING
Short sentences, familiar words, and simple concepts for children eager to read on their own.

READING WITH HELP
Engaging stories, longer sentences, and language play for developing readers.

READING ALONE
Complex plots, challenging vocabulary, and high-interest topics for the independent reader.

ADVANCED READING
Short paragraphs, chapters, and exciting themes for the perfect bridge to chapter books.

I Can Read! books have introduced children to the joy of reading since 1957. Featuring award-winning authors and illustrators and a fabulous cast of beloved characters, I Can Read! books set the standard for beginning readers.

A lifetime of discovery begins with the magical words "I Can Read!"

Visit www.icanread.com for information on enriching your child's reading experience.
Visit www.zonderkidz.com for more Zonderkidz I Can Read! titles.

"Praise the Lord from the earth,

you great sea creatures and all of

the deepest parts of the ocean."

—Psalm 148:7

ZONDERKIDZ

Sea Creatures
Copyright © 2011 by Zonderkidz

Requests for information should be addressed to:
Zonderkidz, *Grand Rapids, Michigan 49530*

Library of Congress Cataloging-in-Publication Data

Sea creatures.
       p. cm. — (I can read!/made by God)
    ISBN 978-0-310-72183-3 (softcover)
   1. Marine animals—Religious aspects—Christianity—Juvenile literature. 2. Creation—
Juvenile literature.
   BT746.S43 2010
   231.7—dc22   2010031104

Editor: Mary Hassinger
Art direction & design: Jody Langley

Printed in China

18 19 20 21 22 /DSC/ 12 11 10 9 8

I Can Read!

···MADE·BY·GOD···

Sea Creatures

CONTENTS

God made everything,

and he made it all good.

He made the birds in the sky

and creatures under the sea,

like the …

JELLYFISH!

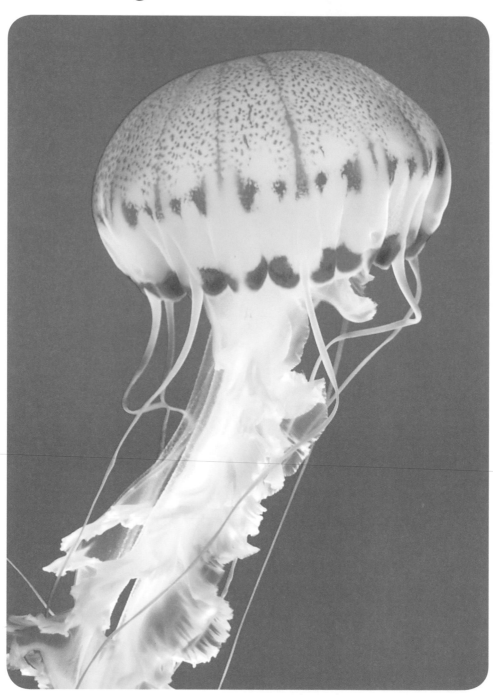

Jellyfish are not really fish.

They do not have bones.

They are more than 90% water.

Jellyfish look like see-through

umbrellas with long legs

called tentacles.

There are more than
200 kinds of jellyfish.
Some are called:
Lion's mane jellyfish
Box jellyfish.
Jellyfish live in groups called
swarms or blooms.

Jellyfish float in the water.

Some move very quickly.

Jellyfish are in every ocean.

Some live near the top;

others live in the deep sea.

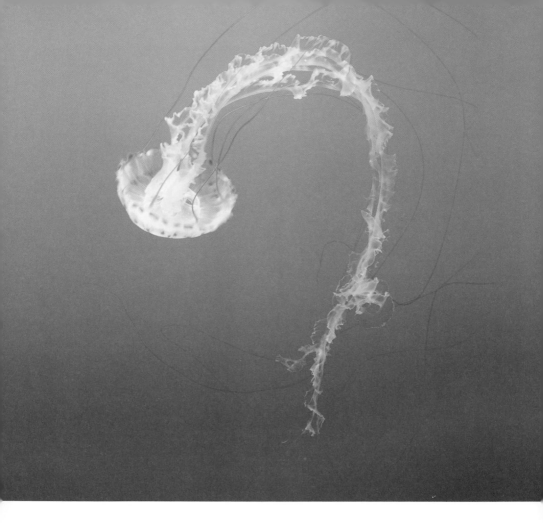

Jellyfish can be huge—120 feet long!

They can be poisonous.

Some of them sting!

Jellyfish only live

two to six months.

Even though jellyfish do not
have brains, hearts, or bones,
they are special to God,
just like …

SEA HORSES!

Sea horses are horse-shaped fish.

There are about 35 different kinds.

They live in shallow, warm,

tropical water.

Sea horses live one to five

years.

They only grow one-half

to fourteen inches long.

Sea horses have to eat almost

all the time to stay alive.

But they do not have

teeth or stomachs!

Sea horses use their tails to
hold onto sea grass so they
can stay still to eat.
They eat plankton and fish eggs.

Sea horses are not good swimmers.

But they have a small fin

on their back

that flutters up to 35 times

in one second.

This helps them move better.

Another special sea horse fact

is that father sea horses

carry their babies

until they are born!

God made many

special sea creatures!

He also made the amazing …

SEA TURTLE!

There are seven kinds of sea turtles.

Some of them are:

Leatherback

Green turtle

Loggerhead

Kemp's ridley

Some sea turtles are in danger.

People do things that are not safe

for the turtles,

like pollute the water.

Even though sea turtles can

live for 80 years or more,

if people are not careful

sea turtles might all die.

Sea turtles live in all of the

oceans, but not in frozen places.

They are almost always under water

but need to breathe air.

When they are swimming,

sea turtles eat jellyfish, seaweed,

sponges, and algae.

Mother sea turtles come out
of the water to lay eggs in the sand.
They lay 50 to 100 eggs, bury them
in sand, and leave.
When the eggs hatch, the babies
run as fast as they can
to get to the water.

The leatherback turtle is the

largest turtle in the world.

It can grow to be seven feet long,

three feet across, and 1,500 pounds.

Leatherbacks live in groups called bales.

They have soft shells.

God made sea turtles so

they cannot pull their heads into

their shells to hide

like other turtles!

God made another undersea creature

so big, they do not have to

hide either … it is the …

WHALE!

Whales are the largest animal
on earth.

They are mammals.

This means whales do things like
breathe air with their blowholes
and have live babies.

There are over 80 kinds of whales.

Some are:

Hector dolphin—the smallest

 at 39 inches,

Blue whale—the largest

 at 100 feet

Humpback whale

Beluga whale

Killer whale (orca)

Whales live in every ocean.

They live in groups

called pods.

They are like a family.

Whales can talk to each other.

They use clicks and pings.

Whales can hear other whales

talk as far away as 100 miles!

Whales can swim fast to get

to each other—30 miles an hour.

God made some underwater
creatures very huge.

He made some very small.

No matter the size or shape
of his creatures,
God made them all amazing!